Published in 2018 by

Russell House Publishing Ltd
The Coach House
Ware, Lyme Regis
Dorset
DT7 3RH

Tel: 01297 443948

e-mail: jan@russellhouse.co.uk

British Library Cataloguing-in-publication.

Data: A catalogue record for this book is available from the British Library.

ISBN: 978-1-905541-99-7

CONTENTS

About the author

Frankie Hudson began her career as a modern language teacher before setting up and managing the UK's first educational unit for school-age mothers in Bristol.

Her experience of the emotional needs of her pupils led her into sex and relationship education with young people, counselling and counselling training. She has a private practice as a counsellor and counselling supervisor.

Alongside her counselling work, Frankie is an artist and mosaicist; she enjoys singing with the Bristol Choral Society and playing the cello. She lives with her husband in Bristol.

Acknowledgments

This little book would not have come about without the encouraging responses of my students and clients who found my quick sketches useful, often enlightening and sometimes life-changing.

Special thanks go to my good friend Toyin Okitikpi, my nieces Megan Hitchcock and Anna Hudson, my nephew Tim Hudson and my husband David Emmerson.

We Can Work It Out
Understanding ourselves and our relationships

by

Frankie Hudson

1
Introduction

We Can Work It Out
Understanding ourselves and our relationships

We are all driven by a quest to make sense of not just the world around us but also who we are, where we have come from, where we belong and what the future holds for us. These fundamental questions manifest themselves in our life in different ways and at different times. However, most of the time we live our lives as best we can without dwelling too much on trying to find answers. There are also times when these questions push themselves to the forefront of our minds and demand that we examine and consider them, even if we are unable to come up with answers. These are universal questions about the human condition; they are not unique to any individual or group of people. The difference arises in our personal approach and how we each understand and experience our curiosity.

There is an on-going discussion in the counselling world regarding which comes first, our feelings or our thinking. I believe we are driven by our feelings. It is certainly true that our thoughts can get in the way of getting on with our life; and of maintaining comfortable and fulfilling relationships. But when we are emotionally aroused our thinking brain shuts down; we then tend to think and behave irrationally.

However, when you have looked through the pages of this book, you can make up your own minds.

There is no road map about how we should live our lives. Our first learning is by imitating the behaviour of those closest to us and how they treat us and each other. As we grow up our lives are influenced and shaped by the people around us, as well as a myriad of other different factors. We make choices all the time, but some situations where we find ourselves are beyond our control. This means that we are unable to make choices or changes. It is important to recognise the difference between what we can do and what is beyond our control.

This little book came about over the years I have spent teaching counselling skills (and theory) at different levels to a wide range of people in many fields of work. These have developed during my own counselling practice. I offer here some ideas about communication, with simple drawings to illustrate the point and which might bring a smile. So this is for everybody who is interested in understanding how relationships work (and maybe don't seem to be working), why we sometimes fail to communicate effectively with each other, and what makes us tick.

Jargon free

My aim originally was to help clarify some rather abstract concepts by means of image and metaphor. Rather than trying to explain a theoretical concept in words, I found that a simple image brought an idea to life immediately, in that it went straight to the heart of our personal experience. I found that an image as a metaphor can often have an impact where mere words fail. For example an image can trigger a memory, produce a 'eureka'/light bulb moment, bring a smile of understanding; invite a sense of meaning where confusion previously kept a person stuck.

So here I offer a simple image to represent an aspect of our behaviour, and alongside a brief written commentary with notes designed to be both helpful and encouraging. I hope it will help some readers make meaningful links with their own way of being in their relationships.

This is not a jargon-filled book. On the contrary, my aim is to reach anyone who wishes to increase their understanding of themselves, and begin to reflect in a gently critical way on why - and how - they react as they do; to have compassion for themselves and others in accepting and respecting their own and others' idiosyncrasies; to thus be less judgmental of themselves and others.

We each come with our own bundle of experiences, expectations, hang-ups, values, prejudices, skills, levels of competence and confidence, etc. It can be difficult keeping an imaginative and open mind if we are burdened or preoccupied in some way. And since we are all unique individuals, no two people will see or grasp an idea in the same way. To make ourselves clear and understood, we need patience to keep trying different ways of saying what we mean or want. It can often take several goes in a variety of ways to explain something before the penny finally drops and it all begins to make sense to us.

As an individual, a couple (or one of a couple) or a family group (or a member of a group), there should be something in this book for everyone that will help shed light on how you feel about yourself and the way you relate to others. And with luck some hopeful sense of how to make changes, if that's what you want.

Life in a sketch

It is almost impossible to take in something new if we are uptight, tense or anxious, or emotionally not present. I have noticed that, when someone hasn't the energy to grapple with the written or spoken word, an idea expressed in a quick sketch, done in a few seconds, can provoke a relaxed and enthusiastic response of understanding and self awareness.

4

If the right conditions are in place, the atmosphere calm, relaxed, honest and friendly, the chances are that we can be open with our feelings and so be free to learn and embrace new ideas. In this way we may become engaged with whatever it is we're struggling with and so make meaningful links with our own lives. In other words, if we can be critically reflective in this way we can become open to and accepting of the lives and struggles of others.

My hope is that these drawings will bring a smile of recognition to you for yourselves. They will also I hope enhance your understanding of the human condition and some of the reasons why we behave as we do. For we generally do not question much unless we find ourselves in difficulties; and once this discovery is made it may be too late to change without considerable help and support. Also you may gain a new perspective on something, which you had previously understood and now see differently.

If we are ready to work towards a change, it's important to have a clear and attainable goal in mind. This is the 'what'. Then comes the 'how', which is the crucial bit. So the 'what' is the idea for action (for change); the 'how' is the means or method. Having made the decision to do something, the 'how' depends on how we feel about ourselves in order to get started. It's about getting back in the driving seat of our life, managing ourselves in the face of whatever difficulties arise; and developing an understanding of our responses to people and events as also theirs to us. Noticing how we are in any given situation can help us understand the other people involved. We cannot change the other's responses; however, we can work on changing ours. Often making a positive change in ourselves enables positive change in others.

Likewise changing our response to events, words or actions will elicit changes in how others receive or 'read' us. For, since we are driven by our feelings, it's likely that they will get in the way of a balanced exchange. As well as listening to what others say, we need also to be able to listen to what we say to others, and how we say it. It is like listening to our own heartbeat, it requires a different kind of awareness.

An important aspect of any relationship is about understanding the limits, the boundaries of how to 'be' in it. If we trust ourselves and feel comfortable in our skin, we are more likely to know whether to trust another or not, and more likely to behave appropriately with that person. If we are authentic – true to ourselves – we offer the chance for others to be so too. That is the best we can do, and it is already a lot. If we want others to change we have to start with ourselves.

It's not about persuading; it's about engaging. We do this by first recognising our way of relating. This self-awareness opens us up to another by inviting and encouraging them to see for themselves how they see the world, and themselves in it; and what they need and want to do to increase the quality of their life. We cannot do it for them, but we can be alongside as they do it for themselves.

Many of us have unsatisfactory relationships which ultimately do us harm. It's not so much the relationships which are harmful, but rather our habits within the relationships which do the damage. At first the potential damage is invisible as we do not see it and don't think to look. Short-term there seems to be no problem, yet sooner or later we may find elements which now seem destructive. We can get stuck in a habit of relating and responding in ways which are no longer appropriate. We do what's familiar because, until we learn to do things another way, we know no better. It's here that we need a little help and encouragement.

And often we resist change.

Knowing, appreciating and even liking and loving ourselves is perhaps the keystone to a fulfilling relationship with another. This book therefore also offers something about maintaining relationships of all kinds in ways that have meaning and purpose for those involved. To my mind there is something distinctly satisfying about setting out with a target for change in mind, and achieving it, however long it takes.

My motto for this is: 'Purpose and Achievement'. Having a purpose is an achievement in itself.

Conclusion

I did not set out to write a self-help book; however, this may turn out to be just that for you. The ideas behind it were more observations than advice; observations which I wanted to share and so shed light on how to help us re-take charge of our own lives. It's not just a question of seeing how we might go about (or 'do') something differently, but also how to 'be' in a new and more effective way.

Another of my mottos is: 'You can't engage with the task until you engage with the person'.

In other words, it's no good thinking we can solve a problem by thinking we can change a behaviour, we need to want to make the change for ourselves, understand and accept why we want to, and then know how to do this; and only then how to practise the new way. And if we are helping another to make changes, before addressing the issue we must first engage with how that person is feeling.

They are more likely to pursue their project with an enthusiastic and open mind if they feel understood, at peace and relaxed.

While ultimately there is very little substitute for seeking the help of a qualified professional, be it a counsellor or therapist, it takes a great deal of courage to make the decision to find the help and support that is needed. However, there are practical steps and some early thinking that could be done in the meantime.

I hope you not only enjoy this book but also find it useful. You may find the order of the ideas confusing or not quite right for you. It's something to dip into perhaps, rather than read from cover to cover.

And may courage and hope go with you.

THE LEARNING GRID

The Four Stages of Learning

unconscious	incompetence
conscious	incompetence
conscious	competence
unconscious	competence

The Four Stages of Learning

One way of understanding how we manage to effect change is to bear in mind how we ever learnt anything in school. If we think back to our school days and the way we sometimes struggled with getting our heads round sums, words, music, poetry, etc. or learning to play an instrument or speaking a foreign language, it's now obvious that the way to achieve our goal is by repetition. We say or do something over and over again until eventually we succeed.

The learning grid explains this. One of the best examples is learning to drive a car.....

What can help?

a) Think back to when you first learnt to drive. Most of us now drive unconsciously competently!

b) What have you recently learnt to do? In all humility, how competent are you? Remember there is always more to learn.

<u>Learning Grid:</u> Developed in the 1970's by Noel Burch, employee at Gordon Training International. Cited in Human Journal Volume 22, no2-2015.pp 40-41.

2

Stuck

BLOCKS 1

BLOCKS 1

When we feel unable to make decisions or move forward it feels as though a great heavy block is in the way. It is like a "millstone round our neck". These heavy burdens weigh us down and stop us from getting on or being our true selves.

What can help?

Start thinking about how to move the block out of the way, even a little way. Draw strength from an area in your life when you have managed to resolve a problem, however small. Relish this achievement and remind yourself:

    a)   that you managed it, and

    b)   how you did that; in other words what personal strengths or skills did you access and use that were helpful.

Even if you can't move it completely, you may be able to stop it blocking out all the light.

BLOCKS 2

BLOCKS 2

Of course blocks come in different guises and some are more visible and can easily be spotted. However, there are others that only become apparent when we stumble upon them unexpectedly. Shifting blocks requires effort.

What can help?

It may be too tough to do this by yourself. Try and make a list of all the blocks that you feel and think are getting in the way, are preventing you from moving forward. What or who are you afraid of? What's the worst that could happen? For it is usually fear that keeps us stuck.

a) Think about what you need in terms of time, resources and support that may lessen the load and the effort required.

b) Choose someone, who has maybe provided support before, to help push these great weights to one side, and one by one.

STUMBLING BLOCK

STUMBLING BLOCK

Stuff gets in the way, holds us back, from a particular task? In day-to-day life?, or simply keeps us procrastinating? We don't know why we can't move on. Or we do know what's stopping us but we can't seem to do anything about it. Whatever it is, we can't face it. We're scared of change; we're used to things as they are, even if we're not happy..... Better the devil we know....?

What can help?

There are of course different ways to help us think around the problems we encounter. See if you can bite the bullet with the following idea:

Think of yourself as captain of a ship. You know where you're heading but you have many tasks to deal with while navigating the unpredictable seas in getting there. Stormy weather, unruly sailors, leaking boat.....You are in charge. You are the navigator. If you need a shipmate, think about who or what kind of person you could trust to be your second in command.

If the above doesn't resonate with you, see if you can find another metaphor for your block. Could you soften it? Squash it? Dissolve it?

Choose a metaphor to suit you.

THE BRICK WALL

THE BRICK WALL

Using metaphors to help us think about the blocks, obstacles and problems in our life can be useful. For example we sometimes say we are coming up against a brick wall when we are unable to find a way through. It feels as though it is impossible to sort anything out because every time we try we meet a brick wall. And we usually find someone else to blame for our inertia, because, let's face it, we find it hard to acknowledge that it might be something to do with us. After all, is the brick wall of someone else's making, or do we put it there?

What can help?

Well, metaphorically, you could take a drill and bore a hole through it; small enough to at least get a glimpse of what might be on the other side.
This might be scary and so:

    a) Asking for appropriate help would be good.

    b) Or imagine finding a ladder to climb up and look over.

You may well find the other side not nearly as frightening as you feared.

EMOTIONAL CONSTIPATION

or

Where do I start?

EMOTIONAL CONSTIPATION
or
Where do I start?

When we hold back from speaking about what feels to be unspeakable, it can take several goes to even begin to say what's on our mind. It can feel excruciatingly uncomfortable and frustrating, for both ourselves and our listener.

We require from our listener much patience and empathic understanding while we try to talk. Sometimes it can be easier to talk to someone with no emotional ties with us; other times it's helpful to have someone who knows a little about what's going on for us.

What can help?

a) Writing down your thoughts by keeping a diary, or writing a letter (which you may or may not send) can help clear your head and give you confidence.
This could be to and/or about anybody, alive or dead.

b) Reading it through can be quite revealing and incredibly helpful.

SPILLING THE BEANS

SPILLING THE BEANS

Sometimes we need to pour out what's troubling us. But letting it out can be both a relief and an embarrassment. We may be profoundly relieved when we have the opportunity to say what we want to say, yet at the same time feel somewhat emotionally and psychologically vulnerable. What will they think of us?

What can help?

It is often true that "I know what I think when I hear what I say". Talking to someone, who has few emotional ties with you would be a good start; someone who would not try to 'rescue' you by offering off-the-cuff solutions as to what you should or shouldn't do.

a) Writing it down can help you hear your thoughts. It may also turn out for you that "I know what I think when I read what I write".

b) Again, keeping a journal can be a way of off-loading safely, and arranging your thoughts and feelings.

SYMPATHY vs EMPATHY

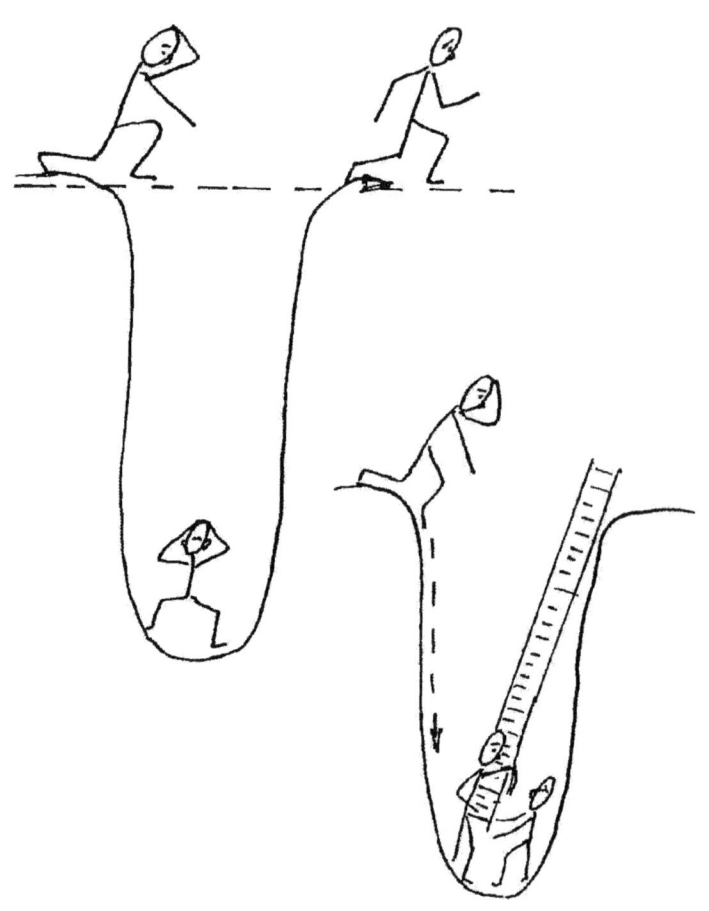

SYMPATHY vs EMPATHY

Sympathy and empathy are often confused and, while they are both about emotional expression and connection to others, each has its own place.

Sympathy is when we feel sad about someone's plight. We express our feelings of compassion and show them in some way that we're thinking of them.

Empathy takes us a step further by making the effort to try and put ourselves in the other person's shoes. If we know someone feels the pits we know they need some empathy. If it's you in the pits you need more than a simple acknowledgement, and **others'** expressions of pity won't help.

What can help?

It's important to remember that trying to rescue someone from their difficulty and impose a solution does not actually work. If you need help, or you know someone who needs help, 'walking alongside' is the way to think about helping another to get out of the pit. So:

a)   If you want to support someone in distress, they need to trust you to be there for them; not to provide solutions or do it for them.

b)   Be open to your own need for appropriate support and encouragement so that you feel motivated to help yourself.

DARE....

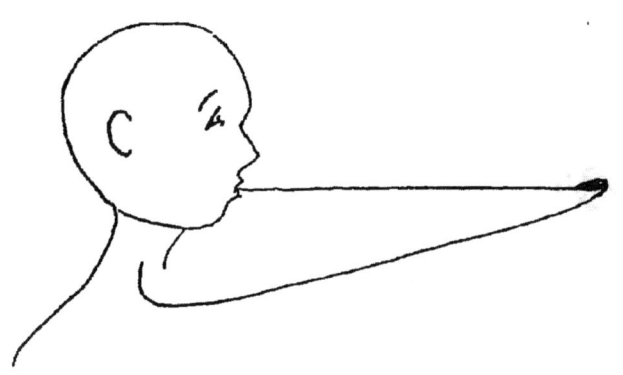

DARE TO STRETCH THE CHEWING GUM TO BREAKING POINT

When we cannot quite bring ourselves to break with a habit we chew it around like a gum and stretch it as far as we can. This could be seen as stretching the chewing gum as far as we can…If the chewing gum represents the issue we're grappling with, stretching it creates tension. Of course it may be that the tension is helpful in driving us on to complete a task. But when stress builds up to a certain point it can be hard to see what's happening and something might snap.

What can help?

Metaphors are useful as they take us a step away from our emotional state, and with luck draw a smile. When we smile, we relax.

a) Find any metaphor that best suits your situation.

b) While too much stress can lead to "break", just the right amount can lead to "make".

THE MASK 1

THE MASK 1

When we feel vulnerable the need for protection and defence can be very strong. We comfort ourselves by thinking that we will be fine as long as we hide our feelings and pretend to be OK.

We believe that if we put on a brave face nobody will know. For example when we are asked "How are you?" we reply "I'm fine". Over time this can become a habit which can be hard to change, and we lose our real self. It's like living a lie, and we can get so used to this that we come to believe our own lie. And yet we might still feel something is not quite right.

What can help?

Trying to please others may be an important reason for the mask. Or you may fear embarrassing others or yourself, and "People won't like the real me".
It may feel crucial not to 'rock the boat' or 'upset the apple cart'.

     a) Better to be true to yourself and ask yourself why the pretence and the mask.

     b) Practise making the effort to notice (to yourself) when you're not being truthful. Incidentally, this might help you recognise it in others.

THE MASK 2

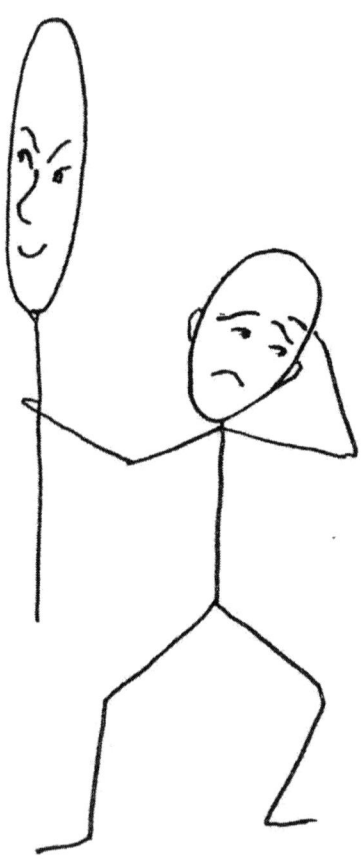

THE MASK 2

The mask acts as our protective cloak. The fear is that allowing it to slip would reveal our true selves to others. This can be scary, certainly different, and so it can feel unnatural, possibly uncomfortable. However, it's worth taking the risk.

Strange as it may seem, pretending uses up a lot of energy; it causes stress and anxiety. Being real and true to ourselves takes less effort.

What can help?

Notice when you find yourself pretending and if possible take a moment to ask yourself why. If you are feeling not too emotional you could maybe stop and think before responding in a situation.

a) When you manage this, notice the effect on others as well as on yourself.

b) Keep practising and responding to others in ways that reflect your true self. Asserting yourself in this way can be uplifting.

THE HOLDING BOWL

The talker has a lot to say.
He can speak freely. The
listener helps by not taking
personally any angry and
emotional outpourings.

THE HOLDING BOWL

When we need to pour out our sorrows and confusions they need a safe place to land. Imagine a metaphorical bowl placed strategically between listener and (agitated) talker. The danger of being either the 'dumper' or the 'dumped on' is avoided, as the 'stuff' remains in the bowl. It is important that the listener doesn't offer advice or comments such as 'Why don't you...?', 'If I were you...' etc., or even butt in with 'I know just what you mean, I had the same experience' and so on.

I call this last the 'Oh well I....' syndrome.

What can help?

The Holding Bowl can be very freeing and a safe container for both parties as neither carries away any emotional baggage.

a) It is crucial to talk to someone who will genuinely listen, not interrupt or offer advice.

b) Keep in mind that the bowl will take all, and both talker and listener will leave the space free of 'stuff'.

ANXIETY BLOCKS PERFORMANCE

ANXIETY BLOCKS PERFORMANCE

We are all driven by our feelings. When we're emotionally aroused, as in frightened, upset, angry, frustrated, worried, anxious, even desperately in love, the thinking part of our brain shuts down. So we respond to people and events without thinking, and this often causes communication breakdown. The result is emotional log-jam. Not helpful to either party.

What can help?

Remember that your responses, both emotional and rational, are your own, no-one else's. Blaming others is unfair and does not work. Our feelings are triggered by events and behaviours, and when we're under pressure – we feel overwhelmed, and anxiety sets in. This means we can't think straight which means we don't function as well as we might.

a) Ask yourself what is causing your anxiety and inappropriate response. When, where and with whom did such a situation happen before?

b) How else could you respond and what would help you? Acknowledge your anxious or angry feelings, then engage brain to deal with the situation.

NEGATIVE THOUGHTS

NEGATIVE THOUGHTS

When we do not feel confident it's often because we are feeling incompetent. This can result in all sorts of bad thoughts about ourselves which only bring us down and even further. The feeling that 'I'm hopeless at...', 'I'll never be able to...' Or 'I can't ...' swirls around in your head. For example, we may not be very good at maths (a common complaint), but we may be a brilliant cook. Unfortunately, it is the 'not good at' feeling that dominates our thinking.

What can help?

Boosting the ego and turning the negatives into positives is not easy. Changing the negative thoughts into positives may require you to unlearn way of thinking which have been preventing you from seeing yourself and your situation in a positive light. Feelings affect thoughts and thoughts affect mood.

    a) Write down only positive phrases about yourself, and keep repeating them.

    b) Talk to others about things you can do. Both these actions will help you to see the difference in your view of yourself and the world.

STICK IN THE MUD

STICK IN THE MUD

The phrase 'stick in the mud' is often associated with someone who is stubborn and who does not want to change; we are happy to stay stuck where we are. However, what is often not appreciated is that we may be stuck because we fear change; as a result we are immobilised by that fear. It is difficult to think about moving forward if we don't know what we are moving towards.

What can help?

Metaphorically, to get unstuck and move forward you may have to grab at the barbed wire fence in order to heave yourself out. This represents your only support in this desperate situation. This action may well be painful, draw blood, strain your arm muscles. You may have to leave your boots behind. Leaving something behind can be a relief as well as sad, but it is part of moving on.

a) Think about your fears and concerns about moving on; write them down.

b) What and who would help you to overcome those fears?

3

Developing Awareness

FEELING INADEQUATE

FEELING INADEQUATE

When we believe we can't do something our sense of competence and confidence blend into a negative blur which can dominate our sense of self. We may well feel defensive in such a situation, and in frustration react aggressively – shout or fight – or passively – creep away – neither of which is rational; the thinking brain has shut down as the anxiety takes over. As always it's the emotional brain that hi-jacks the thinking brain. Understanding the intricate connection between competence and confidence will become evident when we put into practice the learning process.

What can help?

To embark on this, try something completely different. This conscious change teaches us that learning a new habit is possible after only a week of conscious practice

a) Set yourself the task of cleaning your teeth or combing your hair with the other hand, putting on jeans starting with the other leg, or coat starting with the other arm….etc.

b) Transfer this knowledge to trying out new things that you've been wanting to do….

THE EMOTIONAL BIN

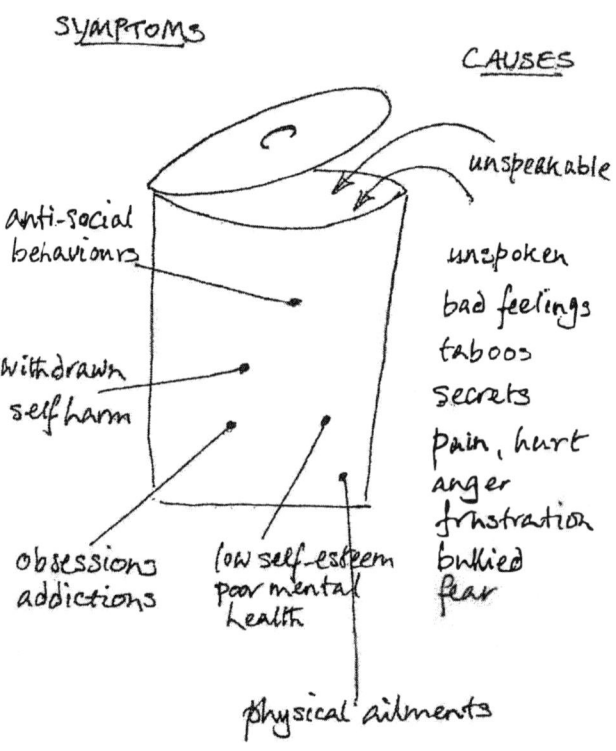

SYMPTOMS

CAUSES

unspeakable

Anti-social
behaviours

unspoken
bad feelings
taboos
secrets
pain, hurt
anger
frustration
bullied
fear

withdrawn
self harm

obsessions
addictions

low self-esteem
poor mental
health

physical ailments

THE EMOTIONAL BIN

Over the years secrets and taboos accumulated from childhood are stashed away from our conscious self and stuffed into our metaphorical bin and the lid firmly shut down. The bin provides a safe hiding place where all difficult negative thoughts and feelings, such as memories, experiences, fears, guilt, anger, jealousy, can be stored out of conscious mind.

In there go all that is 'unspeakable' and 'unspoken', and the lid is tightly rammed down to keep all in: and out of consciousness.

The individual items which went in at the top are no longer recognisable within. All the bad things mix and mingle as they churn around inside. The accumulation of repressed 'bottled up' feelings fills the bin to bursting point. The bin has a finite volume and begins to show signs of stress.

What can help?

Just dealing with the symptoms (the current behaviours) is not enough; it's what went in that needs to be addressed. Ignoring the root cause is like putting a plaster on a deep wound that needs attention first.

a) Do not be afraid of lifting the lid and looking in your bin. You may need someone with empathy and understanding to help you. Start exploring what you have stuffed there.

b) It's important that you begin to accept your bin's contents, and forgive yourself and others for whatever happened in the past which you needed to stuff in your bin.

THE WRONG FIT

 Here I have room to breathe. I am OK. I function well. I am healthy. I feel free.

Here I am, stretched and cramped in ways which prevent me functioning properly. I can't breathe. I feel trapped

THE WRONG FIT

We feel comfortable being a certain way; free to love, like, think, choose, and free to behave with accepted boundaries. We know where we are and feel good. This is where we are healthy in body, mind and spirit.

When others have expectations of us, make assumptions about us; when they make decisions for us based on their wishes and hopes, not ours, we can become so entangled that we are lost. We cannot function properly when the shape or mould they require us to fit into feels wrong. It is a form of bullying. We feel constrained, restricted, hemmed-in. We're very uncomfortable and feel confused, frustrated and angry.

What can help?

Recognising this misfit is the first thing. Perhaps, in going along with others' ways and values, you have lost sight of your 'normal'.

a)   Acknowledge this misfit and check that you are happy with your 'normal'.

b)   Assert yourself, making it clear that their 'normal' is not yours.

BRUSHED UNDER THE CARPET

I'm a nuisance. People walk all over me. Trample on me. I'm flattened.

BRUSHED UNDER THE CARPET

We can often feel invisible, although still in the way of others. We feel dismissed, unseen, ignored, avoided; disbelieved, unheard; perhaps even walked over. Whether it is we ourselves, or our 'stuff', which is getting in the way of others noticing us, it is an uncomfortable place to be. And we possibly make it worse by avoiding encounters when this might occur, as in: pretending that 'I'm not here'. This can be habit-forming.

What can help?

Getting people to notice the real you is not going to be easy.

a) Start by reminding yourself that it is not you, but others' ignorance and lack of sensitivity that causes you to feel and behave as your do.

b) Be assertive. Take a risk. Be courageous and step by step get your voice heard and make yourself visible.

Relationships we make in order to make up for the losses and pain in our formative years.

Childhood relationships and experiences which have dented our ego. We feel unloved.

THE COMPENSATION STRETCH 1

When we feel that our childhood has been lacking in essential unconditional love; when we still feel unwanted, undervalued for some reason; or when things haven't gone smoothly at significant periods of our lives. If we have suffered abuse. If our parents have divorced, or we have suffered significant bereavements...For all these reasons, and many more, we may well make relationships with others and/or with things, to make up for the loss we have experienced. Because of these experiences we are probably unaware of why our relationships are now unsatisfactory.

Such experiences can severely dent our self-esteem and, as a result, we push out, away from the dent, in an attempt to keep the ego-volume stable.

What can help?

a) Acknowledge the unsatisfactory relationships and what it is about them that make them so. Be honest and clear with yourself.

b) Recognise what's going on and try to identify the causes. Think about the extent and nature of what you may want to confront.

THE COMPENSATION STRETCH 2

With help, understanding and acceptance we can begin to repair our ego; retreat from the damaging and inappropriate relationships; and welcome — or at least come to accept — some of our unhappy childhood experiences.

THE COMPENSATION STRETCH 2

All relationships involve a certain amount of compromise which might feel like – but should not involve – losing part of one's identity and true self. However, any loss or change is hopefully compensated for by the gains of being in a relationship. And yet, an unsatisfactory, destructive or dysfunctional relationship causes damage to our self-esteem and to our sense of belonging in the world. In order to withdraw from what's not now working for us in terms of our current relationships – for example, with partners, substance abuse, obsessions – we need to be honest and identify if our life feels as it should be; and also what it is we feel we didn't have in terms of our needs being met in childhood and growing up.

What can help?

With help, understanding and acceptance you can begin to repair your ego: retreat from the damaging and inappropriate relationships, and welcome – or at least come to accept – some of your unhappy childhood experiences.

a) Write down your thoughts and memories of events and relationships which you consider were damaging.

b) Talk about these thoughts and memories with someone who will really listen and not judge you.

THE TYRANNY OF THE PAST

TYRANNY OF THE PAST

When we feel we can't handle a situation or we are frightened of embarking on a task, or simply frustrated and stuck, it's possible that we unconsciously find ourselves in a situation which reminds us of a similar past event where we felt incapable or inadequate; perhaps 'shown up' or uncomfortable, and we don't understand why.

I call this the tyranny of the past because it relates to our previous experiences and seems to come to get us in unexpected moments. In these moments we can find ourselves acting inappropriately.

What can help?

Recognising what happened in the past is important because it helps to place 'now' in its proper context. But we should not let the past hold the future to ransom.

a) Remind yourself: 'That was then, this is now'. Or: 'That was my parent, this is my partner/friend/etc'. The situation may feel similar but these are different circumstances and different people.

b) Question your feelings and be aware of what is going on.

MOVING FORWARD

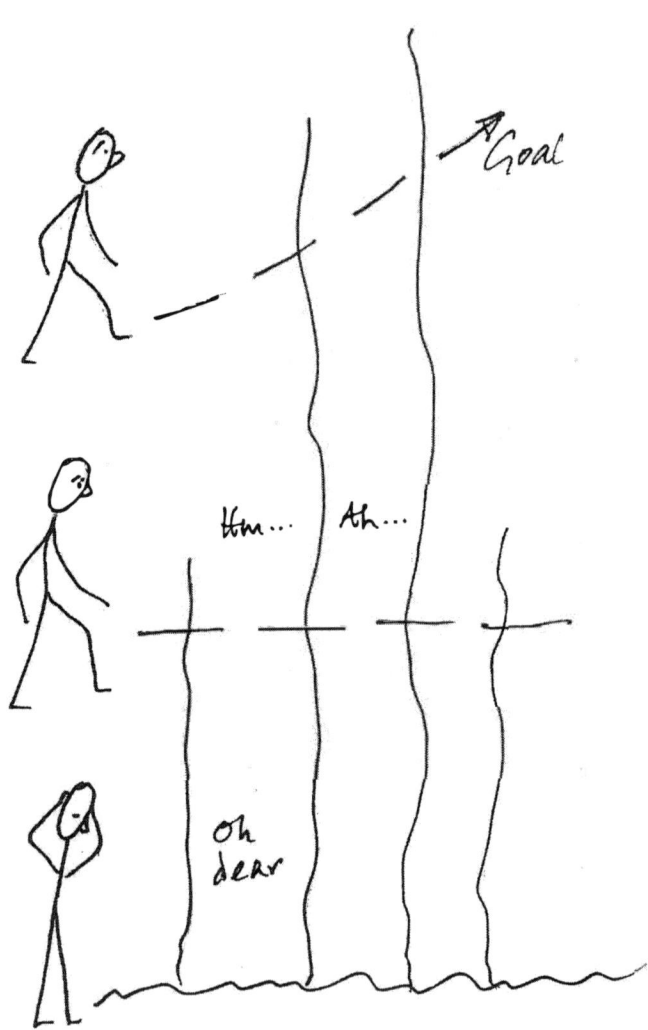

MOVING FORWARD WITH AWARENESS

If we're going through difficult times, depending of course on the nature of the problem, we could simplify the way forward by seeing it in 3 ways.

If it is a practical matter it is possible it can be dealt with, given applied thought and maybe several attempts. If it is to do with how we're feeling, maybe spending time with someone who will genuinely listen is what we need. If, however, our difficulties have their origin in our past experiences, while continuing to haunt us, then the solution required to help us address these may be more complex. Our past can never leave us; however, we can learn to live with and manage it effectively, and so avoid its intrusion in our life today.

What can help?

a) Try and identify those experiences which still intrude today, holding you back from fully functioning in a chosen area.

b) Keep practising acceptance that "stuff happens", that blaming our parents does not help, that they, like us, did the best they could in the circumstances they found themselves in.

MARKING OUR TERRITORY

MARKING OUR TERRITORY

Some people simply have to leave their mark, everywhere they go and in any way they can.

Pandas apparently do this by leaving their scent with total commitment against every tree they pass.

I guess we all know people who just can't help making their opinion known over and over again. And maybe we find ourselves being a bit objectionable in this way too sometimes.

Do trees ever say 'Give me a break!'?

What can help?

Ask yourself why they – or we – need to do this sort of top-dogging. It's usually a far-back-reaching need to be heard, listened to, and at least even noticed.

a) How do you think other people see you? What impression do you think you make on others?

b) How do you leave your mark wherever you go?

BIRD'S EYE VIEW

BIRD'S EYE VIEW

When we're in the middle of a fight, an argument or simply having a hard time with someone, it can be salutary, even enlightening, to imagine ourselves in a helicopter looking down at us. Or imagine we are a bird passing, flying up above us. What do we see? Two people in difficulty? Might we wonder what this is all about? Sometimes an objective view can help us see the ridiculousness of a situation.

What can help?

a) In the midst of a quarrel, if your awareness can click in, try to imagine you're up high looking down. You may be persuaded to turn away from the argument.

b) You may find yourself smiling.

THE STEAMROLLER

THE STEAMROLLER

Far from suggesting we should behave like a steamroller, aggressively and determinedly flattening everyone in sight, this metaphor nevertheless can resonate with us if we feel pressured or bulldozed (another similar machine...) into doing something completely contrary to our nature.

If we find ourselves feeling 'flattened' by heavy persuasion or bullying, this is the moment to take stock of the situation.

What can help?

a) Get out of the way of the heavy machinery. Stand up, speak up; whatever you can do in the moment.

b) Consider how you got to this, and what's 'eating' the other person so that they need to bully.

4

Understanding ourselves in our relationships

THE SEE-SAW 1

An equal relationship
Both have their feet on the
ground.

THE SEE-SAW 1

Our relationships with partners, friends, families, colleagues, even strangers, work best when they are on an equal footing. Mutual respect and a genuine appreciation of each others' strengths and weaknesses are important. Add to these a willingness to listen, and the chances are that the relationship will not only work for both, but will also thrive. Such a relationship means there is trust, so we can meet each other on the same level; we retain our dignity and integrity, we feel good, knowing we are each heard by the other with sufficient understanding and acceptance, if not agreement!

Metaphorically speaking, since only we are in control of the part we are playing in any relationship, we need to keep our feet well and truly on the ground. Thus we are neither dominant nor victim. To remain 'grounded' means being realistic about what to expect from any relationship, and accepting that no relationship is perfect.

What can help?

a) Speak your piece, your view, stand your ground.

b) As a listener be attentive to what the other has to say.

THE SEE-SAW 2

Bully
Aggressor
Top dog
Persecutor

Victim
Bullied
Put down

THE SEE-SAW 2
Power and Control

It is a truism that every relationship goes through ups and downs, however caring and loving the couple may feel towards each other. This is because all encounters we have with each other are laden with historical baggage which informs the way we behave and see things. However, for a relationship to work well, to the mutual benefit of those involved, there has to be an element of give and take as well as appreciation of what each has to offer the other. When a relationship is characterised by one person wanting to show who is boss, for whatever reason, or they are afflicted with the 'top dog' or 'Mr Right' syndrome, it is likely that the other member of the partnership will become the 'underdog' or victim. Similarly we may be afflicted with the 'poor me' syndrome and put ourselves in victim mode, placing the other in 'top dog'. Whether we find ourselves in bully or victim position is entirely our perspective, for the way we see things is our own, and fed by our (past) experiences.

To survive being in such a relationship the 'victim' may develop all kinds of strategies. In some cases they may expect to be physically attacked and/or subjected to bullying, or sexual, psychological or emotional abuse.

What can help?

a) Recognise your default position; ask yourself where you are on the see-saw in relation to the other, and why you put yourself there. Ground yourself to prevent either dominating or submitting.

b) What level of control do you feel you have in certain relationships? What could you do to change the balance?

THE FRAME 1

I am secure.
I understand the rules.
Boundaries are in place.
I know where I am in
     this relationship.

THE FRAME 1

This is a metaphor for the structure within which a relationship can flourish. We all need boundaries; if we understand the limits, and trust that we will be safely held within them, the relationship will grow positively. It is our natural drive to push at the edges of the boundaries as we grow up, whenever and wherever they are presented to us. And yet, paradoxically, while we feel compelled to push against any parameters put in our way, we nevertheless still yearn for and welcome the reassuring presence of a restraining influence. The frame offers consistency, predictability and containment against both known and unknown. It offers security and sets the rules within which we are able to operate.

What can help?

a) Make sure to keep any promises you make; likewise, if the boundary or frame is breached it is important that you carry out any sanction you pledged.

b) Think about how secure you were as a child. What were your boundaries and how did they work for you?

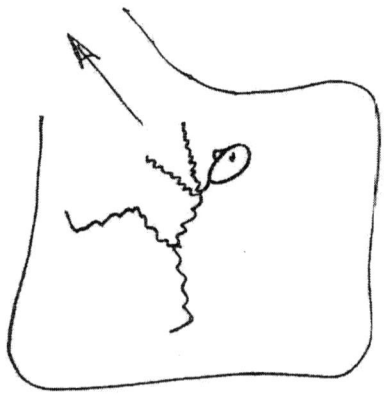

I am no longer safe.
The boundary is broken.
I'm feeling very wobbly. I'm
unsure what's allowed and what's
not allowed.

THE BROKEN FRAME 2

A good enough relationship is one where the centre holds and the loving frame is strong, where there is mutual respect and deep affection and appreciation of each other. When the structure loses its strength, and the frame is broken or comes unstuck, the 'picture' is no longer held securely in place and could fall out. The same applies to a relationship when the boundaries become less clear, the edges fuzzy. We no longer feel secure and can feel unsettled and confused. The relationship suffers, as people no longer know quite where they stand and are likely to escape in some way. This occurs if we do not follow through with any promises and threats we made; we lose respect and dignity, and the subject of our concern will not know how to react.

The need to feel safe and contained is an important part of our childhood experiences which are carried into adulthood.

What can help?

a) Recognising fuzzy boundaries in your or others' relationships is a significant start.

b) What would help to repair a broken frame?

WHY DON'T YOU UNDERSTAND ME?

WHY DON'T YOU UNDERSTAND ME?

We are all individuals with our own peculiarities and personal history. No two experiences are the same. We are made up of the sum of our own life experiences to date, and these are unique to us. Our experiences inform our expectations of our selves, of others, of how things should be done and what is important to us. As a result we view and react to the world in ways which make sense to us, and which reinforce our sense of self in it. No two experiences are ever exactly the same; situations or incidents which we experience may appear similar to the experiences of others, and yet they cannot be the same. Inevitably this leaves us open to misunderstandings. So no wonder we get confused when others don't share our ideas, our opinions, or the 'right' way to do things.

While it is important to recognise that there are similarities in our experiences, it is still important to understand the differences in how we react and deal with them.

What can help?

a) What role does miscommunication play in your relationship(s)?

b) To what extent are you open-minded about other people's expectations of you?

ASSERTIVENESS

In aiming for assertiveness, the passive person can feel aggressive by contrast to his 'normal' self.

ASSERTIVENESS

There is often a misunderstanding of what assertiveness means. It should not be confused with aggressiveness, being bolshie or unnecessarily difficult. Assertiveness is a positive way of being that straddles the middle between passivity and aggression. It is healthy and satisfying to assert ourselves, saying what suits or doesn't suit us clearly and with confidence. Being assertive means having the ability to express and communicate our opinions, views, wishes and concerns in a clear, confident and thoughtful way. It also means not allowing bullying, discriminatory, aggressive or condescending behaviour from others to cause us to wobble.

We could be anywhere on this spectrum, depending on our nature, habit, present mood and circumstances; and significantly how we see ourselves in a relationship.

Like many other behaviours, assertiveness is a learnt response. While some are able to stand up for themselves, others need to learn how to be assertive in an effective and non-destructive way.

What can help?

a) Notice the effect your passivity or aggressivity has on others and watch out for how they respond.

b) Begin to get used to being assertive and note the difference between this and a bully. You could soon get used to standing up for yourself without being a bully. Lovely feeling.

RELATIONSHIP BUBBLES 1

Two separate individuals
clear boundary between
living alongside each other.

RELATIONSHIP BUBBLES 1

One way of seeing being in a healthy relationship is to consider ourselves as individuals existing as separate beings, a clear boundary between us, each retaining our own identity and integrity and self-respect. It is a way of living alongside the other person, not losing touch with who we are, and not getting bogged down in the other's stuff or 'normal' way of being.

This idea could be stretched to embrace other ideas in our lives including our relationship with food, exercise, housework, politics, not to mention our job and other activities, habits and preoccupations.

For a healthy relationship to thrive it is important that the people in it feel comfortable and are willing to listen to each other, and respect differences.

What can help?

a) In your relationships how effective is the boundary between you and the other?

b) How do you enjoy your independence within your relationship?

RELATIONSHIP BUBBLES 2

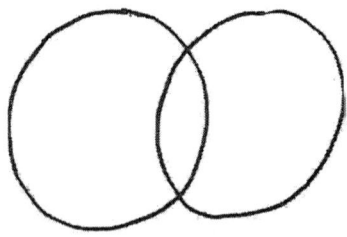

Two individuals choose
to share moments of intimacy
without losing their integrity, or
their sense of self.

RELATIONSHIP BUBBLES 2

Being in a relationship is more than merely being together or living together. A relationship denotes moments of sharing, intimacy, friendship, companionship, caring; and also appreciating and possible valuing the negatives as well as the positives of being together. It does not mean we have to lose our sense of self, our identity or those aspects of our life which are important to us. It is still possible to retain our integrity, our values, our essential self, while linking up closely in whatever appropriate way with the other person in the relationship. Relationship is about making a choice and a conscious decision to join with another.

Learning when and how to disengage from a relationship, or simply an intimate moment, is about asserting ourselves, and treating others, and being treated by them, with respect and consideration for both their and our needs.

What can help?

a) What are your key strengths in the way you manage your relationship?

b) Which aspects of your relationship do you feel you both need to work on?

RELATIONSHIP BUBBLES 3

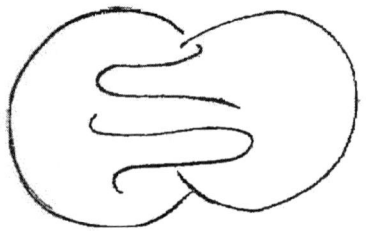

Too much dependence
and entanglement can lead
to losing our sense of self
and our self confidence.

RELATIONSHIP BUBBLES 3

At its best a healthy relationship is where love, care, trust, mutual acceptance and respect are engendered. Those in it feel a bond and closeness that transcends everything else around them. Here personal growth can be achieved as each person feels supported and enabled to achieve whatever they want.

This suggests a certain degree of dependence, and, while this could be a positive attribute, if there is too much dependence and over-reliance on each other it could prove stifling and disabling.

At its most negative it could turn into an obsessive relationship where the individual becomes lost and suffocated in the tangled mess. Self assertion becomes difficult. We begin to doubt ourselves. We could become 'people pleasers'. We begin to lose self confidence, we no longer feel comfortable, and feel trapped. In our anxiety we feel incompetent and can therefore easily make mistakes.

What can help?

a) Take care that you don't allow yourself to get wrapped up in another's way of being (their 'normal') which is not yours.

b) Watch out for being overly dependent on someone or something. Face how this feels, and ask yourself what you might like to change.

Two individuals growing alongside each other.

TWO TREES 1

There are many different ways of characterising the experience of being in a relationship. At its simplest it is about two unique individuals with their own separate roots from which they have grown and learned, and become who they are. They present differently, they look different and they have their own unique character and their own growth history.

They remain well grounded and their roots, integrity and identity feel secure. And yet they can grow comfortably alongside each other.

What can help?

a) If you like drawing, draw the tree that you feel represents you, and another for someone or something you have a relationship with.

b) Have a go at exploring your roots and how they influence you.

TWO TREES 2

Leaves + branches
lean into each other,
may grow towards each other. They
remain well grounded + strong.

TWO TREES 2

Two trees growing side by side may well lean into each other, and blend leaves and branches.

Their trunks remain well grounded and strong in their roots. Their integrity and identity are secure. Their blending with each other from time to time - as the wind takes them? - or being partly attached, does not mean they lose their individual characteristics.

If the branches become tangled up with each other, it can be difficult to distinguish one from the other. It might feel impossible to unravel, as with honeysuckle and bindweed, so a little pruning would be in order.

What can help?

    a) Ask yourself if your relationship needs a little 'pruning'.

    b) If you feel your relationship needs some disentanglement, seek some help in understanding how to do this.

THE NEED TO POSSESS

If we're very needy, the
other person only wants
to run.

THE NEED TO POSSESS

Strangely, in many respects a relationship is more than the sum of its parts. The two people involved bring along not only their recently acquired baggage but also historical legacies, including our childhood memories both conscious and unconscious. Each member of the relationship brings their need for warmth, acceptance, care and a sense of belonging.

The feeling to be cared for can quickly turn into a neediness that damages the trust within the relationship. Being needy can be debilitating. We want someone really badly. Rejection can feel so hurtful and humiliating. We have first to let someone go if we want to keep their love and respect.

The paradox here is that if someone feels free to go, they may well want to stay....The difficulty is letting them go in the first place. This takes courage.

What can help?

a) What is it that compels you to not let someone go? Ask yourself what you fear most if your partner, friend, habit, etc. were no longer in your life?

b) Conversely, if you feel overpowered by another's need for intimacy, how might you deal with that?

GIVING and RECEIVING 1

I don't deserve....

GIVING AND RECEIVING 1
Unable to receive

The art of giving and receiving is not as straight forward as it may at first appear. Sometimes we find it difficult to receive, for example compliments, presents or expressions of affection. We negate, excuse, justify, deny or deflect in order not to show how we feel about receiving. We usually do this because we are embarrassed in some way. While rejecting an offer can cause misunderstandings, it could also be a lost opportunity for closeness. We don't want what is on offer; or we really want it but are too shy or scared to accept.

On the other hand, accepting a compliment does a great deal for the self-esteem of both parties.

As a giver we choose to give for a variety of reasons, but may feel confused and hurt if our generosity or love is not received kindly. We want to be appreciated or at least acknowledged.

What can help?

a) Become aware of your reaction to compliments. Notice how you respond and its effect on the giver.

b) What might be your reason to offer presents, advice or compliments? Who benefits?

GIVING and RECEIVING 2

The need to give.

GIVING AND RECEIVING 2
The need to give

If we want to give, we may well feel confused and hurt if our generosity or love are dismissed. We want to give and it is thrown back in our face. This is uncomfortable for both giver and receiver.

Some people feel an overpowering need to give; this might hide a desire to dominate; to compete; to be loved, be liked, be popular. The expression 'people pleaser' comes to mind. This might work short-term; however, eventually the receiver may lose respect for the giver. Long-term it can be exhausting - and expensive. We shall not get the love we crave with bribes. And this is not how true friendships are made.

What can help?

a) Ask yourself how genuinely generous is your giving? What drives your wish to give? And is your giving appropriate to the situation?

b) And ask yourself about recent offers you have either refused˙ or accepted reluctantly. What were the reasons?

THE NEED FOR SUPPORT

THE NEED FOR SUPPORT

One of the most intriguing aspects of the human condition is our need to be seen, heard and respected as a unique individual who has the free will and capacity to do what is best for our personal development. Paradoxically, at the same time we prefer not to be alone and would like to be supported. These two seemingly contrasting aspects create a tension in us which could both drive us on or hold us back.

This tension can be resolved if we are both willing to trust others and also to let go. Seeking support is not easy since it suggests that not only is there something wrong but also that we are unable to deal with it ourselves.

It is no shame to admit that we all need support from time to time, and especially so when we are affected by a crisis, or stress, illness in the family, a bereavement, etc. However, we may feel too wrapped up in our trouble to ask, or even to let others see our pain. Our experiences may affect how we approach seeking help. We may view seeking help as a sign of weakness. Also we can feel sad when our offer of help is refused.

What can help?

a) How easy is it for you to seek support? What holds you back sometimes?

b) How often do you give support? What form does it take?

BUCKETS 1

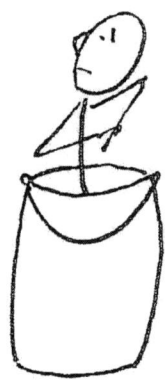 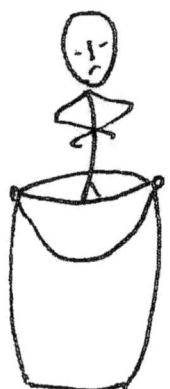

If we insist on sticking to our
point of view; when stepping out
of our bucket means losing face...
we're not even talking to each other?
Why are we so defensive?
What do we fear?

BUCKETS 1

When two people simply cannot agree, when neither is prepared to listen to the other, when there are strong feelings on both sides, it is sometimes difficult to get through the impasse. In such situations we are emotionally aroused so our feelings will have hijacked our thinking and that side of us that is rational and level-headed. Inevitably our capacity to think straight, stand back and understand the other's point of view is lost. Things feel dreadful and we're poles apart; yet our stubbornness keeps us apart. We feel powerless to change the situation and blame the other.

The idea of each of us stuck in a bucket unwilling to step out would draw a smile if it was someone else, and not us. The bucket represents the rigidity of our resistance, our determination not to budge from our standpoint, to 'stick to our guns' whatever the consequences.

What can help?

a) How often do you find yourself in such a bucket? What puts you there?

b) What do you need to do to break the deadlock and step out?

Buckets: **'Peoplemaking' by Virginia Satir 1972, Science and Behaviour Books Inc. USA ISBN: 0 285 64872 1**

BUCKETS 2

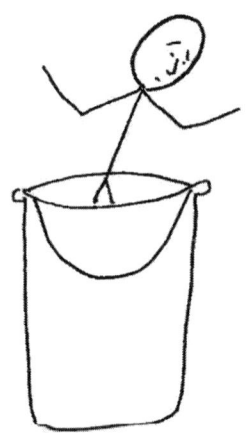 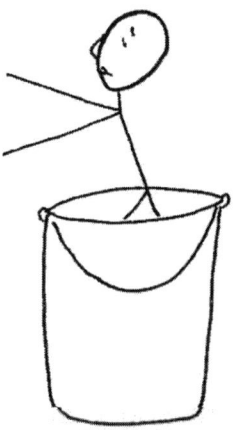

Answering those last two questions
can help us calm down and make
tentative moves to step out of
our buckets.

BUCKETS 2

When we're emotionally aroused – when our feelings have high-jacked our thinking - it's hard to think clearly, and hard to be objective about how we're behaving.

If we can recognise our feelings of hurt, feeling criticised, blamed or attacked, it might help to take a breath, count to five and then break the silence, saying something about how we're feeling. Remember **we** are responsible for **our** behaviour, so we have some influence on the way our relationship goes; we are not responsible for others' behaviour and cannot change it. However, we can influence others with ours.

What can help?

a) Try admitting to your bad or uncomfortable feelings.

b) Ask the others how they are feeling.

BAGGAGE 1

Sometimes we feel as though we're too burdened to carry on...

BAGGAGE 1

If we feel overwhelmed in a way that holds us back, keeps us stuck emotionally somewhere unpleasant, it may well be something to do with our past experiences, possibly our habit of feeling that everything is hard to manage. We may feel so burdened that it is almost too difficult to have a fulfilling relationship with another in an adult way. In fact we keep trying but fail to maintain one for any length of time. Unless we can resolve this in some way we tend to launch ourselves into dysfunctional relationships. Until we see the light.

What can help?

a) How have you become such a burdened person?

b) What is the baggage made up of?

BAGGAGE 2

... and yet we can find
ourselves offering to take on
even more. Such generosity
might appear to help the other
person; it certainly will not
benefit you.

BAGGAGE 2

It may be that we are so used to carrying a lot of emotional weight that we have become unaware of it, since it has been with us as long as we can remember. For example, unfinished business, childhood troubles not addressed, more responsibility than we feel we can cope with. If we continue to carry all this without question or good management we stop functioning well and our thinking can become blocked. In such a case we're continuing in the role of burden-carrier, and could become a burden to others.

What can help?

a) Recognise your limits and be respectful of boundaries – what you can and will take on, and what you know you cannot, and therefore will not take on.

b) Try not to feel responsible for others' burdens. Listen and support without allowing yourself to be dumped on.

BUS ROUTE 1
The Treadmill

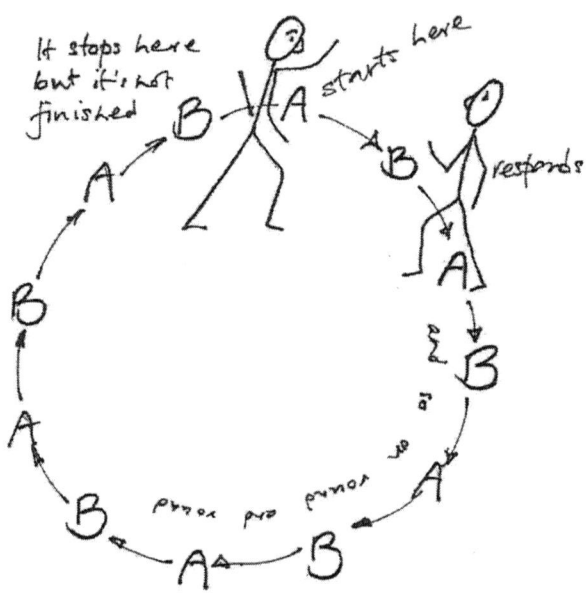

A & B get into an argument over and
over again. The same old stuff comes out.
Each is emotionally triggered by the same
old accusations. Their feelings drive them
relentlessly on, their rational thinking gone.

BUS ROUTE 1
The Treadmill

We can find ourselves in a rut in certain relationships. In such instances we find ourselves locked into a cycle of arguments and conflicts which never seem to get resolved. The physical, emotional and psychological toll to our well-being is immeasurable. It can sap our energy; it can lead to serious depression. When the same issue arises day after day, repeating the familiar cycle of frustration and unfinished business, we are in a cycle of discontent and despair. It feels inevitable.

The idea of the Bus Route helps us to visualise the journey and gives us the chance to choose to get off the 'bus' and take another route, and thus begin a new, or certainly a different, journey.

What can help?

a) What are the triggers that push your buttons?

b) When you realise you are on this bus route, what could you do?

BUS ROUTE 2

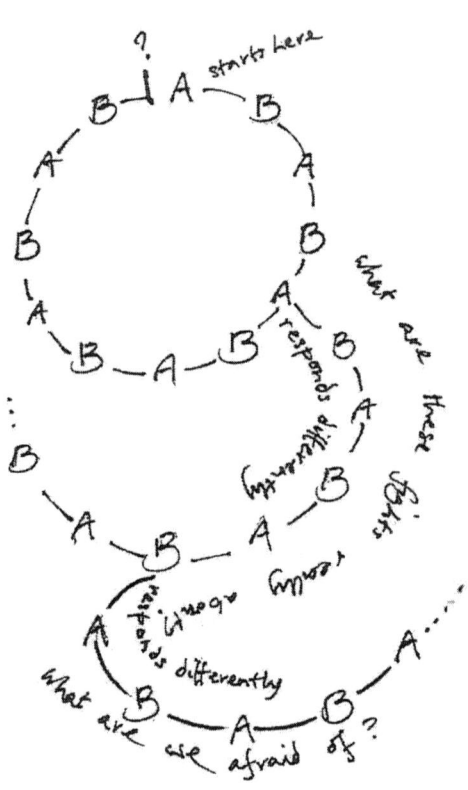

BUS ROUTE 2

When the same old argument starts up again, and we want things to change, recognising what is happening, and making a choice to respond differently is a start. By getting off the bus and getting on another one, our view of things shifts and encourages a new response from the other. Also we begin to feel in charge. Thus the course of the exchange is diverted and altered. A different cycle of exchanges is now in train, and there's a chance now to escape from the old destructive one.

This way of looking at our patterns of responding to one another can help us to become more aware and have more understanding of how and why we misunderstand each other so often, and feel so miserable and helpless.

What can help?

a) Recognise that both of you are on this bus with the set route, and that one of you can get off and change buses.

b) In what ways would things change for you? And for you both?

5

Breaking out into Health

THE LEARNING GRID

The Four Stages of Learning

unconscious	incompetence
conscious	incompetence
conscious	competence
unconscious	competence

THE LEARNING GRID

One way to think about change is to recognise the challenge of learning new ways of going about things. Learning new habits usually means un-learning the old; or at least becoming more aware of them. Above all, it takes courage.

What can help?

Take learning to drive.
We start with: We're not aware there's anything to learn; we're not even thinking about it:

Unconscious   Incompetence

We progress to: Knowing what we want to do and aware that we're not yet very good at it:

Conscious   Incompetence
This is where most of us are some of the time.
This leads to: Recognising that we're doing quite well at this at the steering wheel:

Conscious   Competence
We feel good about this. This is where we are a lot of the time.

And finally: We find we're driving well without much thought. It seems to come naturally:

Unconscious   Competence
We do so much well without conscious awareness. With some things we are still struggling.

Now take one thing you'd like to address for change. Work through the stages and see how you do. The following pages might help.

STEPPING STONES 1

One step at a time
taking care not to lose our
balance.

STEPPING STONES 1

When we recognise a need to change in our life it is sometimes difficult to know what to do, how to do it and where to begin. The easy bit is acknowledging the need for change, the more complicated aspect is bringing about that change. Thinking about it honestly, we may soon realise that how we think about ourselves is at the root of how we behave; how we present – speak, dress, choose our friends and partners – all these aspects and more are what make up how we present and how we are seen by others.

So change would require us to start with our self-perception, for the way we do things is the direct result of our perception of ourselves. Others may interpret us in ways we do not intend. The realisation that something is awry presents the possibility of change. Thinking about this encourages us to make some changes in our behaviour. The way to do this is gradually, step by step. Supportive and constructive feedback on the way is helpful.

What can help?

a) Identify and write down what changes you want to make, with step by step short term goals.

b) What obstacles might be getting in the way of changes you want to make?

STEPPING STONES 2

STEPPING STONES 2

If the stones are too far apart and we're feeling wobbly, the danger of falling is strong. This is why we need short term goals. We may need a helping hand to prevent us from losing balance. We may also need to stand still on one stone while we appreciate each new landing space, and celebrate reaching another short term goal. We can enjoy our new circumstances and take stock of the difference. We also need to take into account that any changes we make can be difficult for others to accept or get used to. It's important to persevere. We can take time to get used to our new way of being, which might feel strange at first, before moving on to the next stage.

What can help?

Remembering that we can only change ourselves, and that changing others is not in our gift

a) What kinds of support would be helpful to keep you on target?

b) Take note how your new behaviour is received by others, and whether their response to you changes (though maybe not immediately), and how long this takes.

TORTOISE SHELL

TORTOISE SHELL

Life does not progress in a straight line, and sometimes small steps can take us forward in a blinkered way. So when we feel bogged down with too many worries to be able to think straight, instead of the usual 'To Do' list, the idea of a tortoise shell with different segments, possibly randomly drawn, presents us with an image. We can fill each segment with as many difficulties, tasks or commitments as we want to include, and without a sense of priority.

The image offers a sense of freedom to choose. And it may be that our of that choosing we find we have after all prioritised. In this way we find relief in knowing where to start. After this random exercise a list may well emerge.......

What can help?

    a) Find your own image to help identify the tasks weighing you down. Your heap of tasks could be fruit or blossom in a tree for example.......

    b) How did you decide what to include? And what happened (or changed for you) in the whole process?

STRESS vs REWARDS 1

STRESS vs REWARDS 1

Stress is caused by many different factors and its impact can be devastating to our confidence and our ability to get on with everyday life. The feeling of being overwhelmed by commitments, pressures, others' demands, and our sense of inadequacy can be so all-encompassing that we lose perspective and find it hard to function. At its worst we may find everything just too difficult to cope with. Disentangling what is truly dreadful from that which is irritating and annoying is not straight forward. We experience stress in our own unique way. It is personal and subjective; it is only through empathy that others can fully comprehend and appreciate our experience of it

What can help?

a) Try to rationalise what is really causing you stress. Maybe you feel a list or tortoise shell coming on.....

b) Compare all those things which you find stressful with what is really good in your life. You may find this a revelation.

STRESS vs REWARDS 2

STRESS   REWARDS

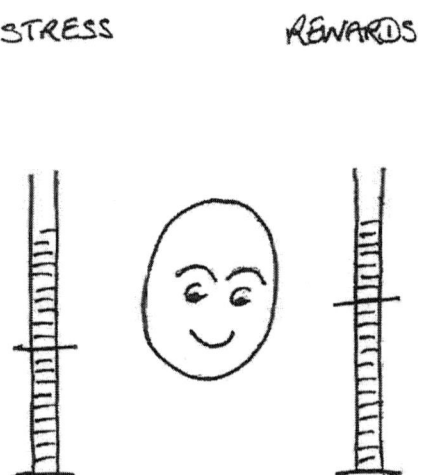

STRESS vs REWARDS 2

We know it is impossible to live a completely stress-free life. In fact a certain degree of stress is important for our existence or we'd never get out of bed! However, it is the nature of the stress as well as its volume and frequency that cause the problems. If stress factors mount up with no sense of rewards as counterbalance, then a negative outcome is inevitable, be it physical, emotional and/or psychological.

Yet if the level of stress compared with the level of rewards is more or less equal, this at least can be a comfort. We can continue to function well, and we can reassess our evaluation of our circumstances.

If, however, the stress level is higher than the rewards, it is perhaps evident that some thinking needs to be done to relieve some of the stress.

What can help?

a) Which stress factors do you have control of and which do you have no control of?

b) How do you contribute to the stress levels in your life? What could you change?

UNPACK THE BAGGAGE

Getting rid of what we no longer need to carry

UNPACK THE BAGGAGE

When we are aware that the emotional baggage is weighing us down, we need to find a way of metaphorically exploring its contents and emptying out any stuff that doesn't belong to us. Or maybe that which does belong to us which we now want to off-load.

We cannot help but be vessels of our parents' way of being and seeing things. Our childhood life experiences with our parents or carers have a profound effect on how we develop as adults. Recognising which bits of our baggage belong to them and which bits belong to us can be a good start to shedding the load. We are so much of our parents' values and experiences that separating what is our and what is their legacy is not easy.

Much of what our parents have left with us may well be an advantage and some of it may be burdensome and irrelevant to our lives today. Working through all this can be tough so a little help may be desirable.

What can help?

a) Try writing a letter to someone significant whose baggage you feel you are carrying.

b) Try physically enacting the handing back of this baggage. For example, placing parents' stuff in a metaphorical sack and then throwing it away can be a relief.

EMPTY THE BIN

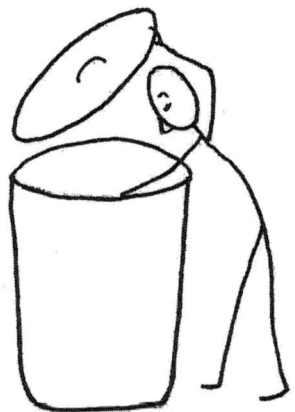

EMPTY THE BIN

Same principle. Same idea. Whichever metaphor resonates with us is the one to use. We may need help to do this, but looking inside and identifying what is buried in there can surprise us. Sorting and chucking out can be a bit like doing the housework, or maybe a spring clean, and throwing out the rubbish. Or like de-cluttering, getting rid of those things we no longer need or indeed want. That was then, this is now..... Remember there was no malice on our parents' part in passing on their learning and experiences. They, like us, only go by what has been handed down to them. And we, like them, can only do the best we can, given the circumstances of time, place, situation and our current relationships.

What can help?

a) If you were to treat this exercise like spring cleaning, what would it feel like? A sense of achievement when done?

b) Knowing that your parents and carers did their best in their circumstances, how can you accept and forgive the baggage while celebrating the positives?

TAKE UP THE BATON

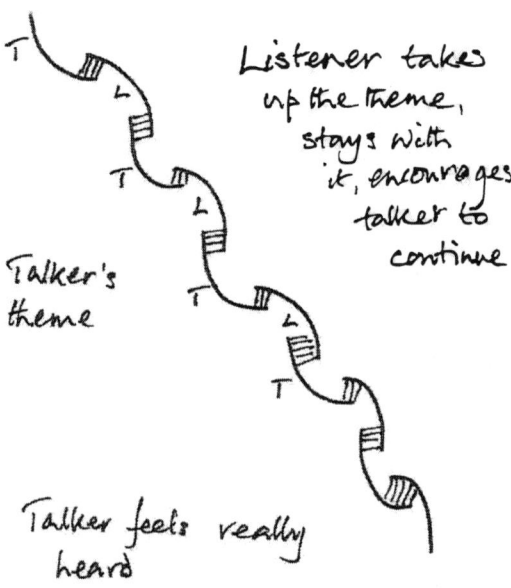

Listener takes up the theme, stays with it, encourages talker to continue

Talker's theme

Talker feels really heard

TAKE UP THE BATON

When we need to off-load we need someone to really give us the time to talk without being interrupted. Each time we pause for more thought it can help when our listener comes in with a response which stays with our theme.

When this happens we can pick up where we left off and also continue with new impetus. This is the best, most comforting and most effective way of conversing with someone when we need a sounding board.

Finding a non-professional person who will really listen and provide the necessary help and support may be too much to ask for. While it is possible to talk to a trusted friend, the danger is that revealing such personal information may change the power balance and the nature of that friendship.

What can help?

a) Try to be as honest and as true to yourself as possible when talking

b) As a listener, make sure that you are active, not passive, in that you stay with the talker's theme or agenda.

AGENDAS

AGENDAS

When people around us see us in pain, they feel the need to help us get over our pain in the only way they know how. Trying to convey sympathy, they may say: "I know exactly how you feel". Although their reaction is understandable, it is not usually helpful. When we are hurting we feel alone; we find it hard to believe that anyone else could be going through the same thing. What we need most is for them to stay with our 'agenda', our story, and not interrupt us with their own. We need them to listen to ours! Of course this is not easy, because people want to make everything alright and for us to be back to our untroubled self. It is often not appreciated that helping people who are going through difficult times requires a great many skills. Active listening and guided conversations are not normally the way people encounter each other. Usually our agendas overlap so that neither party gets to talk deeply about anything. Often this is fine; but not if we need to share something difficult. If we are required to listen, we need to really stay with the talker's story. If we have a similar experience to share, we must wait our turn.

What can help?

a) As a talker, be clear with your listener what you would like from them.

b) As a listener, listen to your talker actively, brushing away, or 'parking' your own related experience. Then it can be your turn.

THREE WAYS.....

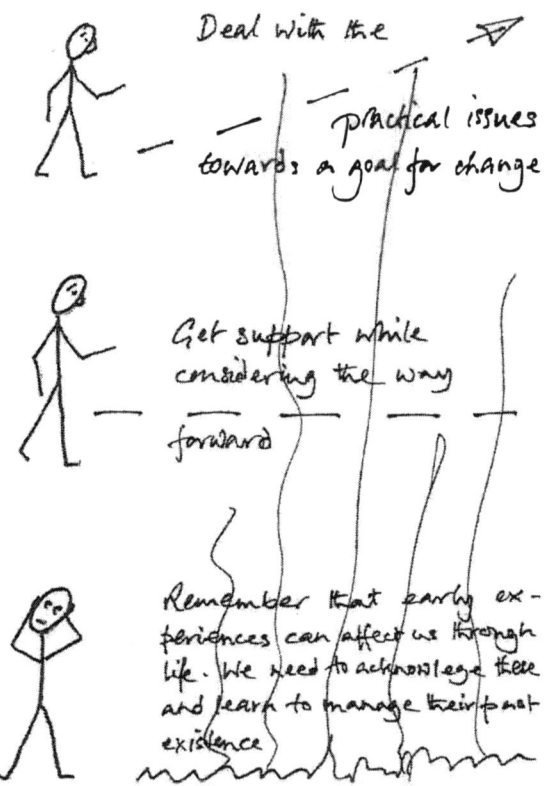

Deal with the practical issues towards a goal for change

Get support while considering the way forward

Remember that early experiences can affect us through life. We need to acknowledge these and learn to manage their past existence

THREE WAYS TO LOOK AT HOW TO DEAL WITH OUR DIFFICULTIES

Often when things are not going well, and we need some help in addressing what's not working for us, it is very difficult to see anything that is positive in our life. It can feel as though nothing we do is right; no-one understands how we are feeling; those around us seem to make matters worse; and even the one area in our life that would normally provide us with solace is of no comfort.

It is at times like this when we are at a low ebb that we may need some help in addressing what is not working for us. We all have our different ways of coping, and dealing with our difficulties as they arise.

There are many approaches to helping us work through our troubles, some more helpful than others, depending on our personality and the nature of our problem.

What can help?

a) Sort out whether the problem or difficulty is practical; if so, what steps might you take to put things right?

b) If the problem is not so clear-cut, then consider using someone as a sounding board. Talking and sharing a problem will help you explore and find your way to clarify, to greater self-awareness and to more satisfactory relationships.

Well? What do you think?

THE SERENITY PRAYER

Grant me the Serenity to accept the things I
cannot change.

The Courage to change the things I can.

And the Wisdom to know the difference.

Reinhold Niebuhr – (1892 to 1971)